People in the
Rain Forest

Saviour Pirotta

RAINTREE
STECK-VAUGHN
PUBLISHERS
The Steck-Vaughn Company

Austin, Texas

Deep in the
Rain Forest

PEOPLE in the Rain Forest
PREDATORS in the Rain Forest
RIVERS in the Rain Forest
TREES AND PLANTS in the Rain Forest

Title page: A ten-year-old boy outside his house in the Amazon. His house has walls made of sticks and mud.

Contents page: A hunter in the rain forests of Madagascar

Published by Raintree Steck-Vaughn Publishers, an imprint of Steck-Vaughn Company

Printed in Italy. Bound in the United States.
  3 4 5 6 7 8 9 0 03 02 01

Library of Congress Cataloging-in-Publication Data
Pirotta, Saviour.
People in the rain forest / Saviour Pirotta.
    p.   cm.—(Deep in the rain forest)
    Includes bibliographical references and index.
    Summary: Describes the people who live in the rain forests around the world, how they hunt and farm, and their religions, festivals, food, and medicine.
    ISBN 0-8172-5137-5 (hard); 0-8172-8111-8 (soft)
    1. Human ecology—Juvenile literature.
    2. Rain forests—Juvenile literature.
    3. Human ecology—Tropics—Juvenile literature.
    4. Ethnology—Tropcs—Juvenile literature.
    5. Tropics—Social life and customs—
Juvenile literature.
    [1. Human ecology. 2. Rain forests. 3. Ecology]
    I. Title. II. Series.
GF54.5.P57 1999
304.2'0913—dc21   97-48525

Contents

Rain Forests around the World

Rain forests are thick forests in parts of the world where there is lots of rain. Most of them are near the equator, an imaginary line that runs around the center of the earth. The biggest rain forest is the Amazon, in South America.

◀ A rain forest family's tree house in Sri Lanka

▼Asmat people in Indonesia

EQUATOR

◀ This boy lives on the island of Madagascar.

■ The green areas on the map show rain forests.

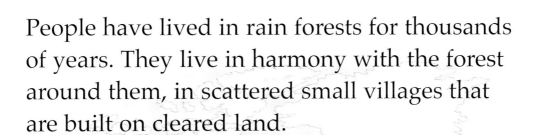

People have lived in rain forests for thousands of years. They live in harmony with the forest around them, in scattered small villages that are built on cleared land.

◀ Cofan Indians in the Amazon rain forest in Ecuador, dressed for a special occasion.

▼This Jivaro man lives in Peru.

▲ Kayapo people live in the Amazon rain forest in Brazil.

Rain Forest Homes

Rain forest people build their homes by using materials they can find nearby. The Yanomani people live in the Amazon. They build enormous huts called *malocas*. Many families share one *maloca*.

▲ Hammocks are cool and comfortable to sleep in.

Yanomani people live together like one big family. They help one another with work like cooking and growing food. Every family in the *maloca* has space where family members can sleep and keep their belongings.

◀ The roof of the *maloca* is made of the leaves of palm trees.

Tree and stilt houses

Some rain forest people live in tree houses. They climb to them, using steps made from the branches of trees.

Many rain forest houses are built on stilts. They keep dry when the ground is flooded.

▲ Houses built on stilts in Papua New Guinea

 8

▼ This tree house in Sri Lanka protects people from elephants.

Hunting and Farming

Rain forest people are experts at hunting and gathering food. Some hunt with spears or with bows and arrows. Others blow poisoned darts through long, bamboo pipes. Many people fish from dugout canoes on the rivers.

▲ A boy in Papua New Guinea using a bow and arrow to shoot fish.

10

Many different animals are hunted for food. Monkeys, birds, tortoises, and wild pigs are favorites. Cane rats, caterpillars, and snails can be tasty, too.

At the end of the day, the hunters bring home their catch to roast on the fire.

▲ A hunter in Madagascar using a sharp spear

Farming

A girl peeling a manioc root in the Amazon

Rain forest people grow only what they need in the rain forest, without causing damage. They clear small patches of land near their homes and grow crops such as manioc, corn, sweet potatoes, bananas, and nuts.

Since the soil is poor, the plot is changed every two years. Then the old farmland becomes rain forest again.

▼ Kayapo women carry home a harvest of corn.

Food and Medicine

Rain forest people hunt or grow most of the food they eat. Manioc is a vegetable that is eaten by most rain forest people. It can be eaten in many different ways.

People grate and pound manioc before roasting it. Manioc flour can be made into bread or pancakes.

▼ Manioc pancakes and meat wrapped in banana leaves cooking on a huge frying pan

◀ A Kayapo man in Brazil with a tortoise ready to be cooked

Sometimes people cook piracuru, which is a giant fish that lives in the Amazon. Its tongue is so hard that it can be used to grate manioc. Tortoises and wild pigs are also very popular. Their meat is wrapped in banana leaves and smoked over a low fire.

15

▲ A Ceram man in Indonesia using a leaf called a devil's leaf to treat his friend's rheumatism.

Medicines

Many natural medicines grow in the rain forests. Rain forest people know more about them than anyone else in the world. The medicine man's herbs can cure many things from upset stomachs to deadly snake bites.

Some rain forest people collect the medical plants and sell them at market stands. The plants and knowledge about them are very valuable to people all over the world. The medicines often reach many different countries.

◀ A Dayak woman in Borneo picks the leaves of a plant called lia lamut. The leaves cure skin diseases and act as painkillers.

Religion and Festivals

Rain forest people have one of the oldest religions in the world. They believe that the world around them is full of spirits, which live in the water, the hills, and the streams.

The shaman is the most important person in the village. He knows how to contact the spirits.

◀ A shaman with a crown of feathers and string of birds that have died. They show that he can contact the spirit world.

▲ Asmat men in Indonesia honoring a sago tree with a special ceremony

Rain forest people believe the spirits look after people by making sure the crops ripen and the hunting is good. So the people take care of the forest around them to keep the spirits happy.

▲ The Kayapo people in the Amazon have painted their faces and bodies to do this special dance.

Festivals

Sometimes rain forest people have festivals to honor the spirits or to ask for their help. Hunters often dance so they will catch better prey. They paint patterns on their faces and bodies.

◀ Hudoq people in Indonesia at their rice-planting festival

The Hudoq people in Indonesia do a special dance at rice-planting time, to ask the spirits for a good rice crop. They wear huge masks and robes made of banana leaves.

▼ Cofan people in Ecuador wearing costumes for a special festival

People in Danger

Many rain forest people have lost their homes and their hunting grounds because the rain forest is being destroyed. Big logging and mining companies are chopping down all the trees.

▼ A tin mine in the Amazon

This family has been ▶
made homeless because
a logging company has
taken away their land.

The trees are sold to countries such as
the United States, to make furniture.

More forest is destroyed as people from
the cities and large companies burn vast
areas of forest for houses and farmland.

Diseases

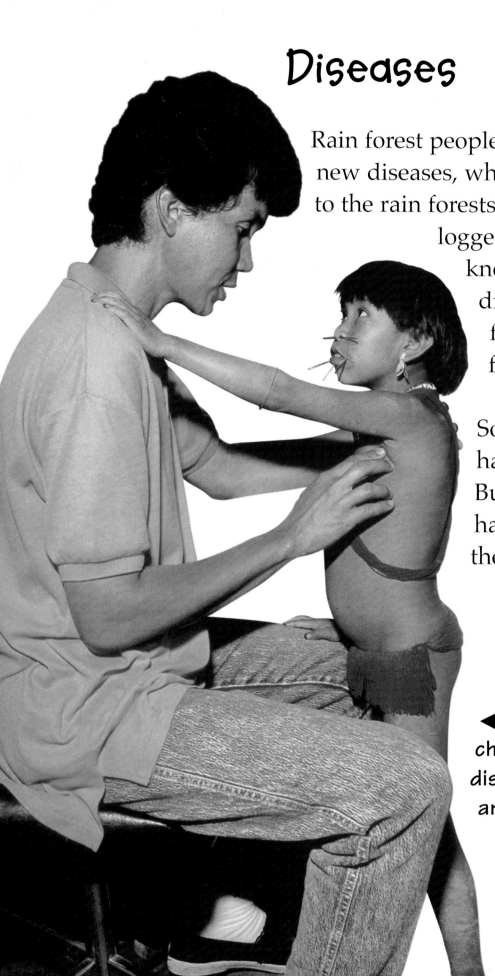

Rain forest people are suffering from new diseases, which have been brought to the rain forests by miners and loggers. The people do not know how to cure these diseases, so doctors from outside the rain forests have to help.

Some rain forest people have begun to eat sugar. But since many do not have toothpaste as well, the sugar rots their teeth.

◀ A doctor in the Amazon checks a child for an eye disease brought to the area by gold miners.

▲ Rain forest people being taken to work in the mines

As rain forest people lose their hunting grounds, they have to find other work. Many people work in the mines for very low wages.

The traditional rain forest way of life is disappearing. If this happens, the valuable knowledge of rain forest peoples will be lost forever.

▲ Dayak people in Borneo block a road to keep logging trucks from destroying their land.

Fighting back

Some rain forest people are fighting back. They are protesting to their governments to stop people from destroying the rain forest.

Some, like the Yakuna group in Colombia, have won their lands back. They can make sure that the rain forest is saved forever.

Finding out more

We can learn a lot from rain forest people. Many tourists can now visit the rain forests. They can learn about the forests from the people and find out about their struggles.

If more outsiders know about the people of the rain forests, they have a better chance of survival. You can help by finding out as much as you can.

▼ This American boy is being taught how to play some pipes by a rain forest chief in Peru.

Face Painting

Before a celebration, many rain forest people paint their faces with colorful patterns. Copy one of the patterns shown opposite or design your own rain forest pattern.

YOU WILL NEED:

● A friend to be your model.

● Water-based face paints: red, yellow, and purple. You can get these in many craft stores.

● Brushes: 1 thin (for drawing fine lines) 1 thick (for drawing thicker lines).

● Sponges: for filling in big areas.

● A T-shirt: make sure it's okay to get paint on it.

● An adult: don't start face painting without an adult there to help.

HANDY HINTS

● Start with simple patterns. People's skin is quite rubbery and hard to draw on. It's best to get used to it before you do a complicated design.

● If you want to try some more patterns, you can find them in photographic books about the rain forest.

WARNING!

Brushes are sometimes thin and sharp. Be VERY CAREFUL if you're painting someone else's face especially if you're painting near the eyes.

1. This man is from the Tara Huli people in Papua New Guinea. Use a brush to draw the outline of this pattern first. Then color it in, using a sponge.

2. This Jivaro man is from the Amazon rain forest in Peru. Use a thin brush to copy this pattern.

3. This pattern is on a Yanomani girl in Brazil. Start this pattern from the bottom of one cheek. Copy it up the side of the face and over the forehead to the bottom of the other cheek.

Glossary

Amazon A region or rain forest in South America around the Amazon River.

Corn A cereal crop, with large ears of yellow seeds growing on tall stalks.

Crops Plants that are grown for food, including wheat, corn, and rice.

Logging Cutting down trees so that the wood can be sold.

Maloca A type of house used by the Yanomani people, in Brazil.

Manioc A root vegetable that grows under the ground.

Minerals Substances like oil, coal, or metal that mining companies dig from the ground.

Painkillers Medicines that help reduce pain.

Protesting Arguing strongly.

Rheumatism A disease causing pain and stiffness around the joints.

Ripen Become ready to be harvested or eaten.

Shaman A special person in the rain forests who is able to contact the spirits.

Spirits Invisible forces.

Further Information

Books to read

Grupper, Jonathon. *Destination—Rain Forest: Rain Forest*. Washington, DC: National Geographic, 1997.

Lewington, Anna. *Antonio's Rain Forest*. Minneapolis, MN: Carolrhoda, 1993.

Lewington, Anna. *Atlas of the Rain Forests*. Austin, TX: Raintree Steck-Vaughn, 1997.

Nagda, Ann Whitehead. *Canopy Crossing: A Story of an Atlantic Rainforest*. Norwalk, CT: Soundprints Digital Audio, 1997.

Osborne, Mary Pope. *Afternoon on the Amazon*. (First Stepping Stone Books). New York: Random House, 1995.

Ross, Kathy. *Crafts for Kids Who Are Wild About Rainforests* (Crafts for Kids Who Are Wild About). Brookfield, CT: Millbrook Press, 1997.

CD Rom

Exploring Land Habitats (Wayland, 1997)

Useful addresses

All these groups provide material on rain forests for schools:

Earth Living Foundation
P.O. Box 188
Hesperus, CO 81326
(970) 385-5500

Friends of the Earth
1025 Vermont Avenue NW
Suite 300
Washington, D.C. 20005-6303
(202) 783-7400

Reforest the Earth
2218 Blossomwood Court NW
Olympia, WA 98502

The World Rainforest Movement
Chapel Row
Chadlington
Oxfordshire OX7 3NA
Tel: 01608 676691

World Wildlife Fund
1250 24th Street NW
P.O. Box 96555
Washington, D.C. 20077-7795

Picture acknowledgments
Bruce Coleman (Alain Compost) 4 (top), 5 (left), (Luiz Claudio Marigo) 14, (Alain Compost) 16, 19, 21 (top); Sue Cunningham Photographic Library *Title page*, 6, 13, 20, 23, 25; Getty Images Limited (Art Wolfe) 29 (middle); Impact (Caroline Penn) 8; NHPA (Daniel Heuclin) *Contents page*, 4 (bottom), (Karl Switak) 10, (Daniel Heuclin) 11, 15; Oxford Scientific Films (Aldo Brando) 18; Edward Parker 12; Planet Earth Pictures (Pete Oxford) *Cover*, 5 (top), 21 (bottom); South American Pictures (Index Editora) 29 (bottom); Still Pictures (Mark Edwards) 5 (right), 7, 9, (Nigel Dickinson) 17, (Mark Edwards) 22, 24, (Nigel Dickinson) 26, (Michael Doolittle) 26 and 27; Trip 29 (top). Border and folio artwork: Kate Davenport. Map pages 4–5 and artwork page 6: Peter Bull

Index

Page numbers in **bold** show there is a picture on the page.

32